COAST NEW ZEALAND

Photographs © Ted Scott, 2016
Text © Catherine Wells, 2016
Typographical design © David Bateman Ltd, 2016

Published in 2016 by David Bateman Ltd
30 Tarndale Grove, Albany, Auckland, New Zealand
www.batemanpublishing.co.nz
ISBN 978-1-86953-934-4

Book design: Catherine Wells
Photographs: Ted Scott, Fotofile Ltd
Printed in China by Everbest Printing Company

CONTENTS

Previous page: Kayaking, Abel Tasman National Park
Left: Archway Islands, Wharariki Beach
Next page: A local tour boat is dwarfed by a cruiseliner, Otago Harbour
Pages 6–7: Mahia Peninsula

INTRODUCTION

Coast Discover New Zealand, a follow-up to *Discover New Zealand*, is a pictorial journey around the country's stunning coastline, from Cape Reinga in the north to Stewart Island in the south. New Zealand is a long, narrow island nation, separated into two main islands by Cook Strait, with Foveaux Strait dividing the country's third biggest island, Stewart Island, from the South Island.

When Maori (the first humans) arrived here in the 13th century they found a landscape covered from shore to shore with dense forest which acted as a barrier to inland settlement. In the 18th century, when Europeans arrived, they too founded settlements on the coast, close to river mouths and in the natural harbours around the New Zealand coastline. Today the major cities of Auckland, Wellington, Christchurch and Dunedin have deep-water harbour access, along with the smaller cities of Tauranga, Gisborne, Napier and New Plymouth in the north and Timaru in the south.

The length of the coast, at approximately 15,000 kilometres, and its reach from a latitude of 35° in the north to 47° in the south gives it huge diversity. The North Island's Pacific east coast, from Northland south to Auckland, offers safe haven to the many sailors and fishermen who frequent this area. These safe anchorages are created by the many islands that act as a buffer against the open ocean; the most famous being the Bay of Islands and the Hauraki Gulf. In contrast, the west coast is more boisterous; here the Tasman Sea and southerlies combine to produce ideal surfing conditions down to Taranaki, and Piha on Auckland's west coast is world famous for its surf-related sports.

Much of the South Island's northern coastline is made up of the Marlborough Sounds, formed from ancient flooded valleys, this is a popular sailing destination, with many islands and sheltered waters. Large sections of the South Island coast have no large safe harbours, especially on the West Coast, until you reach the UNESCO World Heritage Area, in the south-west, which includes Fiordland National Park, an its awe-inspiring landscape of forests, mountains and glacial fiords, where the Tasman Sea penetrates deep into the steep dramatic terrain. On the east coast, the deep water harbours of Banks Peninsula and, further south, Otago Harbour, service the major cities of Christchurch and Dunedin while Bluff serves as the port for Invercargill and is also the sea link to Stewart Island.

Explore and enjoy.

Ted Scott, Karekare 2016

TOP OF THE NORTH

At the end of the road in the Far North is the famous Cape Reinga lighthouse, but it's not quite the most northern point of New Zealand. Looking from the lighthouse east across Piwhane/Spirits Bay is the North Island's most northern point, Hikurua/de Surville Cliffs. To the west is Cape Maria Van Diemen and Motuopao Island. To north, where the Tasman Sea and Pacific Ocean meet, is the Columbia Bank maelstrom, where at times churning waves erupt in explosions of spray.

At the northernmost tip of Cape Reinga/Te Rerenga Wairua is a gnarled pohutukawa tree, believed to be over 800 years old. From here, according to Maori legend, the spirits of their deceased leap to begin their return to their ancestral homeland, Hawaiki.

View east across Piwhane/Spirits Bay to the Hikurua/de Surville Cliffs in the distance.
Above: Pohutukawa at the tip of Cape Reinga/Te Rerenga Wairua

Cape Maria van Diemen, the westernmost point of the North Island

Cape Reinga/Te Rerenga Wairua, and the lighthouse that has stood there since 1941

NORTHLAND/ TE TAI TOKERAU

Nowhere in subtropical Northland is more than 40 kilometres from the coast. In the west, running north from the massive Kaipara Harbour, is Ripiro Beach, New Zealand's longest drivable beach, with the famous Ninety Mile Beach (which is only 88 kilometres, or 55 miles, long) further north again. Between them is the picturesque Hokianga Harbour.

The more irregular east coast is scattered with myriad islands and indented with many harbours. From the north is Parengarenga Harbour, boasting the brilliant white sand of Kokota Spit; long, narrow Houhoura Harbour; wide, shallow Rangaunu Harbour; and the beautiful Whangaroa Harbour. Then there is the internationally renowned Bay of Islands, a popular tourist destination, and, further south, Whangarei Harbour, with Bream Head marking the entrance.

Numerous offshore islands dot this coastline, including the Cavalli Islands to the north-east of Matauri Bay. The main island of the group, along with the world-famous Poor Knights Islands, 50 kilometres east of the mainland, and the Hen and Chickens Group are all nature reserves and a permit is required to land.

Northland is also known as Te Hiku-o-te-Ika, 'the Tail of the Fish'. In Maori oral history, this land formed the tail of the fish that Maui hauled up from the depths of the ocean that became the North Island/Te Ika a Maui.

Whangaroa Harbour

HARBOURS AND BAYS

1 Kerikeri Stone Store, Bay of Islands
2 Land yachts, Ninety Mile Beach
3 Houhora Harbour
4 Pataua North, Ngunguru Bay
5 Pahi, northern Kaipara Harbour

Cruise ship, Bay of Islands

Cavalli Islands from the Kauri Cliffs Golf Course

Entrance to Hokianga Harbour

Elliot Bay, just south of Cape Brett

Mt Lion at the end of Bream Head from Uretiti Beach

HAURAKI GULF /
TIKAPA MOANA

On the doorstep of Auckland, New Zealand's largest city, are 4000 square kilometres of sparkling water scattered with more than 50 islands, forming the Hauraki Gulf Marine Park. The park includes the Waitemata Harbour, Firth of Thames and eastern coastline of the Coromandel Peninsula.

Close to the city and dominating the skyline is volcanic Rangitoto Island, which emerged from the sea just 600 years ago. Further east is Waiheke Island, with a population of almost 8000, it is known for its vineyards and restaurants, and is a popular day trip for Aucklanders. Further the north, is historic Kawau Island, a short ferry trip from the mainland.

In the gulf there are many islands with sheltered bays and harbours, many providing safe moorings whatever the weather for the thousands yachts and launches owned by Aucklanders. Some islands are conservation areas and have restricted access, and they are integral to maintaining and enhancing the biodiversity of the region. A showcase of these islands is the open sanctuary of Tiritiri Matangi, just off Whangaparaoa Peninsula, north of Auckland. Here, visitors can see many unique New Zealand native birds that no longer survive on the mainland, including the iconic takahe.

Auckland CBD with wharfs and the historic customhouse building in the centre. Manukau Harbour (see page 30) can be seen in the distance

SPORTS ON THE WAITEMATA HARBOUR

1 Kayaks circle a swimming platform
2 Yacht race, with Little Barrier Island on the horizon
3 Westhaven Marina
4 Annual summer swim series at Kohimarama Beach, with Rangitoto Island dominating the background
5 Dragon Boat Race finish line
6 Maori waka, Waitemata Harbour, with Rangitoto behind

Kayaks head out, looking towards Rangitoto, from Arkles Bay, Whangaparaoa

Yachts racing in the annual Auckland Anniversary Day regatta

View from North Head on the North Shore over Torpedo Bay towards Auckland city
Next page: Evening, Waitemata Harbour

ISLANDS IN THE GULF

1 Mansion House Bay, Kawau Island

2 Yachts race off Rangitoto Island

3 Tranquil moorings, Waiheke Island

4 Pakatoa Island

5 Little Barrier Island wildlife sanctuary

Tawharanui Regional Park, a mainland island sanctuary of beautiful white sandy beaches, farming and pest-free habitat for threatened native wildlife

MANUKAU HARBOUR

To the west of Auckland is the Manukau Harbour, New Zealand's second largest. Constantly changing sandbars and the rapid tidal flow through the narrow mouth between the heads can make navigating the harbour challenging. Historically, it was an important waterway for Maori, providing portages to the Waitemata Harbour and the Waikato River. The bush-clad hills of the Manukau also had vast stands of kauri, a valuable timber and a vital part of the early New Zealand economy.

The shore is lined with extensive mudflats and mangrove swamps, providing a habitat for migratory birds such as the bar-tailed godwit, turnstone and lesser knot. The threatened New Zealand dotterel and godwit and other birds (pied, little, and black shags, terns, kingfishers and white-faced herons) make their homes here year round.

The waters of the Manukau are a nursery for several varieties of shark. Mullet is caught here on a commercial level and recreational fishers catch snapper and flounder, while shellfish can be found on the shoreline and sandbanks. The highly threatened Maui dolphin, the world's smallest, can sometimes be seen between the Manukau Harbour and Port Waikato further south.

Pied shags on the Manukau Harbour

Cornwallis wharf

Opposite: Manukau Heads

IRON SAND BEACHES

At the edge of the rainforest that clads the volcanic Waitakere Ranges west of Auckland is a stunning wild coastline, where the Tasman Sea meets the shore. Over time, volcanic sand has mixed with magnetic iron oxide ash to form the distinctive black-sand beaches of Auckland's west coast.

At the northern head of the Manukau Harbour entrance is Whatipu Beach. The shifting sand dunes constantly change the beach-scape and caves that were once reached only from the beach are now accessible from a walk through the wetlands.

Further north are the famous surf beaches: Karekare, made known to the world in the film, *The Piano*; Piha, watched over by majestic Lion Rock; and the smaller Bethells Beach (Te Henga). A walking track crosses the northern headland to secluded O'Neill Bay, another favourite with surfers.

At Muriwai Beach, the Takapu Refuge Gannet Colony is home to approximately 1200 pairs of nesting birds each summer, best seen between August and March. The 60 kilometres of beach at Muriwai is designated a public road and is a wonderful place for fishing, horse riding, swimming and surfing.

A golden end to a day at Bethells Beach

Lion Rock, Piha
Opposite: The Cauldron, Karekare

Gannet fly past, Muriwai Beach

Sand dunes, Te Henga/Bethells Beach

Whatipu, at the southern tip of the Waitakere Ranges
Next page: Spectacular west coast sunset, Karekare Beach

COROMANDEL

East of Auckland the Coromandel Peninsula juts into the Pacific and forms the eastern limit of the Hauraki Gulf. A mountainous spine divides the peninsula into two distinct parts. On the west coast there are wetlands and scenic stony bays, and on the east coast are some of the best white-sand beaches in the North Island.

Mercury Bay on the eastern coast was named by Captain James Cook during his expedition to observe the transit of Mercury in 1769. The Maori call it Te-Whanganui-o-Hei, 'the great bay of Hei'. The mouth is 10 kilometres across, and within the bay is the resort town of Whitianga, and the well-known beaches of Wharekaho (Simpsons Beach), where ancient pohutukawa trees, some of which were described by Captain Cook, stand; Cathedral Cove, with its famous stone arch and natural waterfall shower; Hahei; and Hot Water Beach. The bay is also known widely for its yachting and as a step-off point to big game fishing off the coast.

Towards the southern end of the Coromandel Peninsula are the holiday towns of Tairua and Pauanui, where visitors sail, kayak and windsurf in the sheltered Tairua Harbour. Beach fishing and surfing are also popular from the nearby ocean beach.

Cathedral Cove

Dawn, Wharekaho (Simpson Beach), Coromandel

COROMANDEL PENINSULA

1 Tairua
2 Kuaotunu Beach
3 Kayaking, Mercury Bay
4 Whangapoua Harbour

BAY OF PLENTY AND EAST CAPE

The Bay of Plenty, *Te Moana-a-Toi*, stretches from the foot of the Coromandel Peninsula to Cape Runaway on East Cape. The 259 kilometres of coast opens to the Pacific Ocean, and the bay has many scattered islands, including the actively volcanic Whakaari / White Island, and Tuhua/Mayor Island and Motuhora Island, both of which are wildlife sanctuaries.

The Port of Tauranga is the economic hub of the region and one of busiest ports in New Zealand with over 1500 cargo and cruise ships arriving throughout the year.

At the southern end of the bay is sunny Whakatane, where a bronze statue celebrating the bravery of Wairaka sits atop Turuturu Rock. When the waka (voyaging canoe) *Mataatua* first arrived at Whakatane, after making a perilous voyage from Hawaiki, the men went ashore leaving the women alone in the canoe. When the canoe started to drift out to sea, Wairaka (defying a tapu that forbade women handling a canoe) seized the paddle and brought the waka back to shore crying, 'Kia whakatane au i ahau' – 'I will act the part of a man.'

East Cape is perhaps the least well-known coastline in New Zealand. At the headland known as *Te Kuri-a-Paoa*/Young Nicks Head, Captain Cook first sighted the New Zealand coast naming the place after the ship surgeons boy Nicholas Young. It is where New Zealand's longest wharf was built in the 1920s and where Gisborne is the first city in the world to see the sunrise.

Cruise ship, Tauranga

Whakaari / White Island

The lunar landscape of the inner crater on Whakaari / White Island

COASTAL TEXTURES

1 Driftwood, Whanganui
2 Strata, Cape Colville
3 Seaweed, Stewart Island
4 Shells, Castlecliff, Whanganui
5 Golden kelp, Piha
6 Bird tracks, Karekare
7 Sand patterns, Te Paki, Northland
8 Volcanic rocks, White Island

Bronze statue of Wairaka, Whakatane Heads

Camping, Wharekura Point, East Cape

Wharf at Tolaga Bay

Young Nick statue, at the mouth of the Turanganui River, Gisborne

Feeding stingray on the Reef Ecology Tour, Tatapouri Bay

Gisborne City

HAWKE BAY

Hawke Bay is a large semi-circular bay that extends 100 kilometres from the Mahia Peninsula in the north to Cape Kidnappers in the south and gives its name to the Hawke's Bay region. Mahia translates to 'murmur', and the beautiful full name, Te Mahia mai Tawhiti, means the 'murmuring of home'. The mild climate of the Mahia Peninsula makes it popular for surfing, fishing and diving.

Located at the south of Hawke Bay is Napier, a popular tourist destination and well known for its Art Deco buildings. It is also the main port for the Hawke's Bay region.

Cape Kidnappers, home to the world's largest mainland gannet colony, is a craggy peninsula named by Captain Cook after Maori traders seized his Tahitian cabin boy, who they thought was being held against his will. When Cook's men fired on the Maori canoe, the cabin boy escaped and returned to the ship.

Cliffs along the Mahia Peninsula

View to the Mahia Peninsula from Waikokopu

Evening yacht race, Napier

TARANAKI AND WHANGANUI

The dramatic snow-topped volcanic cone of Mount Taranaki, and its surrounding foothills, juts into the Tasman Sea half way down the west coast of the North Island. In the Maori language, Taranaki means 'gliding peak'. As the story goes, Taranaki once lived with the North Island's other great volcanoes (Tongariro, Ruapehu and Ngauruhoe), but was banished for falling in love with Tongariro's wife, Pihanga. Taranaki fled west towards the setting sun, carving out the Whanganui River as he went.

On the long curve of coastline to the north of the mountain, in the North Taranaki Bight, near Tongaporutu, you can see two 25-metre rock formations known as the Three Sisters. At the turn of the 20th century there were four 'sisters', but the sea is claiming them one at a time. South of the Three Sisters, is the deep-water port city of New Plymouth, New Zealand's 'oil town', known for its arts scene, public gardens and black-sand surf beaches.

Whanganui, in the South Taranaki Bight, is a 19th-century river-port city at the mouth of the Whanganui River.

Ko au te Awa, ko te Awa Ko au

I am the river, the river is me.

Originally used by local Maori, these lines have come to symbolise the spiritual relationship between the river and all those whose lives are intertwined with it.

Three Sisters, Tongaporutu, Taranaki

FISHING NEW ZEALAND'S COAST

1 Lone fisherman, Auckland
2 Sulphur Point, Tauranga
3 Fishing from kelp-covered rocks, Piha
4 Fishing site popular with humans and gannets, Muriwai
5 Fishing at dawn, Houhora

Lee Breakwater, New Plymouth

Whanganui City, at the mouth of Whanganui River

Driftwood sculpture, Castlecliff Beach, Whanganui

1 Cape Foulwind Lighthouse, Westland
2 Waipapa Point Lighthouse, Southland
3 Boulder Bank Lighthouse, Nelson
4 Farewell Spit Lighthouse, Tasman
5 Bean Rock Lighthouse, Auckland
6 Katiki Point Lighthouse, Moeraki Peninsula, Otago

LIGHTHOUSES

There are three categories of 'lighthouse' used around the New Zealand coast:
landfall lights, the first to be seen by an approaching vessel; coastal lights, not only used for
fixing and confirming a vessel's position but to warn of rock and reefs; and harbour lights,
such as Bean Rock light in Auckland's Waitemata Harbour, which guide ships safely into port.

Cape Egmont Lighthouse, Taranaki
Next page: Castle Point Lighthouse, Wairarapa

WELLINGTON HARBOUR/ TE WHANGANUI-A-TARA

Bounded by a line between Pencarrow and Palmer heads and north to the Petone foreshore, the enclosed 89 square kilometre Wellington Harbour has many sheltered bays and beaches. Within the harbour there are rowing clubs, waka ama clubs and many yacht clubs, and wind surfers and water-skiers have plenty of space outside the commercial shipping lanes.

Restored wharves and cargo sheds provide a spacious and entertaining pedestrian-only waterfront reserve next to New Zealand's capital city. Here locals and visitors can enjoy Maori carvings, memorial plaques and artworks, as well as Te Papa Tongarewa (the national museum), theatre, galleries, restaurants and cafés.

Houses above Oriental Bay, Wellington Harbour

BOAT HOUSES

1 Evans Bay, Wellington
2 Totara North, Whangaroa Harbour, Northland
3 Ngapipi Road Boat Sheds, Hobson Bay, Auckland
4 Robinsons Bay, Akaroa Harbour, Canterbury

The Boatshed, Taranaki Street Wharf, Wellington waterfront

PORTS

1 Fergusson Container Terminal, Auckland
2 New Plymouth Yacht Club, Port Taranaki
3 Port Chalmers, Otago
4 Lyttelton Container Port, Canterbury
5 Eastland Port, Gisborne
6 South Port, Bluff Harbour, Southland
7 Port of Tauranga, Bay of Plenty

Wellington CBD and Harbour from Mount Victoria

TOP OF THE SOUTH

The northwestern coast of the South Island is a wild place. There are massive cliffs at Cape Farewell pounded by the Tasman Sea, and white sand dunes, islands and caves at Wharariki Beach lead into the distinctive long sand spit that is Farewell Spit. Following the coast from Puponga in the west to Pohara in the east, is Golden Bay/Mohua, with a string of truly golden fine-sand beaches. The next 120 kilometres of shoreline forms the V-shaped Tasman Bay/Te Tai-o-Aorere, the westernmost point of which is located in the picturesque Abel Tasman National Park, also renowned for it golden sand, but also for its granite cliffs, forest-fringed beaches and world-famous coastal track.

Grey Cliff on the Tasman Sea shelters the northern reaches of the Whanganui Inlet

Archway Islands, Wharariki Beach, Tasman

Oyster catchers and black-backed gulls, Puponga, Golden Bay

Morning light, Whanganui Inlet, Tasman

Abel Tasman National Park

Kayaking, Abel Tasman National Park

Kaiteriteri, Tasman Bay

Evening, Tahunanui Beach, Nelson

MARLBOROUGH SOUNDS

Queen Charlotte, Kenepuru and Pelorus Sounds, the Tory Channel and countless bays, inlets, reaches, channels, islands, islets and rocks make up the Marlborough Sounds, which accounts for fully one-fifth of New Zealand's coastline. According to Maori tradition, the South Island is the canoe *Aoraki*, and its sunken prow forms Queen Charlotte Sound / Totaranui and Pelorus Sound / Te Hoiere.

Within this sea-drowned valley system are several predator-free islands providing sanctuary for endangered native wildlife, including kiwi, tuatara, native frogs, giant weta, saddleback, takahe, geckos and the vulnerable New Zealand king cormorant.

In earlier times, the sounds provided shelter and food for Maori. The low saddles between the sounds created portage ways, allowing them to carry waka, or canoes, without the need to travel through to the open sea.

At the head of Queen Charlotte Sound / Totaranui, is the town of Picton, a major transport hub for road and rail and where ferry services between the North and South Islands have their terminals.

Dawn over the Marlborough Sounds
Next page: Waikawa Bay, Marlborough Sounds

Picton Marina, Marlborough Sounds

Queen Charlotte Sound / Totaranui, Marlborough Sounds

KAIKOURA

The Seaward Kaikoura mountains, part of the Southern Alps that run much of the length of the South Island, come close to the coast at Kaikoura, providing a stunning backdrop to the township. Offshore, several species of whale can be seen at different times of the year, with huge sperm whales generally seen year-round. The rich coastal waters are also home to a host of other marine mammals and bird life, including dusky dolphins, fur seals and albatross making a stop in Kaikoura a must-do for nature watchers.

Kaikoura's other famous attraction is crayfish (rock lobster). The Maori name Kaikoura translates to 'meal of crayfish', kai meaning food and koura, crayfish. The plentiful food attracted Maori to the area and, later, European whaling stations were briefly established. The remains of several pa sites and whaling stations can be seen on the Kaikoura Peninsula south of the town. Maori legend tells us that Maui placed his foot on the Kaikoura Peninsula to steady himself while he 'fished-up' the North Island (Te Ika-a-Maui, or the fish of Maui).

Pohutukawa, beachfront, Kaikoura township

COASTAL BIRD LIFE

1 Red-billed gull, Bluff
2 South Island pied oystercatchers, Miranda
3 Variable oystercatchers, Coromandel
4 Royal albatross, Otago Peninsula
5 Gannet colony, Muriwai
6 New Zealand dotterel, Karekare
7 Shag colony, Punakaiki

Seal colony, Ohau Point, Kaikoura

BANKS PENINSULA

Just south of the main South Island city of Christchurch is Banks Peninsula, formed from the craters of two extinct volcanos which have created the harbours of Akaroa and Lyttelton, and the many smaller scenic bays that indent the coastline. Nestled in Akaroa Harbour is the historic French and British settlement of the same name, renowned for its colonial architecture. On the northern coast, the port town of Lyttelton is linked to Christchurch by a road tunnel that runs through the Port Hills.

On the southern coast is tiny settlement of Birdling's Flat, situated near the pebble beach that is part of Kaitorete Spit. The beach is well known as a place to find small agates and a variety of other attractive rounded pebbles.

In the Banks Peninsula Marine Mammal Sanctuary, the rare Hector's dolphin, upokohue, is protected, and small pods can usually be seen in and around Akaroa Harbour. Further along the coast, north of this harbour, is Flea Bay, the site of Pohatu Marine Reserve, protecting all marine sea-life, including the white-flippered penguin, korora, which, along with some yellow-eyed penguins, breeds here.

Akaroa Harbour

95

Sumner Beach, Christchurch

Gemstone collector, Birdling's Flat

Dry dock, Lyttelton Harbour
Next page: Evening, Akaroa

OTAGO COAST

Diverse and beautiful, the Otago coastline is dotted with small fishing and holiday communities and stretches almost 470 kilometres from the Waitaki Fan in the north to Wallace Beach in the south. On Koekohe Beach is an interesting geological feature known as the Moeraki Boulders, a group of very large spherical boulders, some of which weigh several tonnes and are up to three metres in diameter. Further south, Karitane near the mouth of the Waikouaiti River is renowned for its golden beach.

The Otago Peninsula shelters the 20 kilometre-long Otago harbour, home to Port Chalmers, Otago's only commercial port, and Dunedin City. The peninsula is renowned for its wildlife: Taiaroa Head is the only mainland colony of royal albatross in the Southern Hemisphere, and the endangered yellow-eyed penguin/hoiho, blue penguins, New Zealand sea lion and communities of wading birds also make the peninsula home.

Maori legend tells that the Moeraki Boulders are the remains of calabashes, kumaras and eel baskets that washed ashore after the legendary canoe, Araiteuru, *was wrecked at nearby Shag Point/Matakaea.*

Hoopers Inlet, Otago Peninsula

101

Evening, Karitane, Dunedin

Otakou, Otago Peninsula

Bleached willow tree, Taieri Beach

Moeraki Boulders, Koekohe Beach

Surf beach, Waldronville, Otago

SURFING

1 Surfer, Taranaki

2 Woman surfing at Aramoana, Dunedin

3 Surf lesson in the rain, Mt Maunganui

4 Women's surf boat race, Piha

5 Surf City, Piha

RUGGED SOUTHERN COAST

Nugget Point, one of the most well-known landforms on the southern Otago coast, is a steep headland surrounded by The Nuggets, wave-eroded rocks are reminiscent of the gold nuggets. Continuing south, extending from Waiparau Head in the Catlins to Awarua Point, at the north end of Big Bay, in Fiordland, and including Stewart Island/Rakiura, the Southland coastline is 3400 kilometres long and hugely diverse.

The most southerly place of the South Island is the wind-lashed Slope Point, where the trees are forever twisted and bent by the prevailing Antarctic winds. Just a few kilometres from Invercargill, the southernmost town in New Zealand is Bluff, world famous for its oysters.

Riverton/Aparima is the oldest permanent settlement of Southland and one of New Zealand's oldest towns with main street's quaint, old-fashioned shopfronts an attraction.

New Zealand's third largest island, Stewart Island/Rakiura, is 30 kilometres from the South Island, across the notoriously rough Foveaux Strait. A large part of the island, 85 percent, is set aside as a National Park and is a haven for brown kiwi/tokoeka, which outnumber humans and are seen day and night, and other native birds. The island has only one settlement, Oban, at Halfmoon Bay and just 28 kilometres of road, but 280 kilometres of walking tracks!

Nugget Point Lighthouse, Otago
Next page: Windswept trees, Slope Point

Coastal sign, McCrackens Rest, overlooking Te Wae Wae Bay on the Southern Scenic Route

Approaching storm, Foveaux Strait

Oban, Stewart Island/Rakiura

Thule, Stewart Island/Rakiura

FIORDLAND

Of the fourteen fiords in Fiordland National Park, the most well known and most accessible is Milford Sound. On its shoreline is the distinctive Mitre Peak/Rahotu, reputedly one of the most photographed peaks in New Zealand, although with 200 rain days a year it is likely be shrouded in cloud.

Luckily when it rains in Fiordland you are rewarded with thousands of temporary waterfalls tumbling down precipitous bush-clad slopes. There are two permanent waterfalls, Stirling Falls and Lady Bowen Falls, which can be seen without taking a boat trip and at 162 metres is the highest fall in Milford Sound.

Fiordland was recognised by the United Nations in 1986 when it was made a World Heritage Area and Fiordland National Park was described as having 'superlative natural phenomena' and 'outstanding examples of ... the earth's evolutionary history'. In 1990 the Te Wahipounamu World Heritage Area was extended to include Fiordland, Westland and Mt Cook National Parks.

Mitre Peak, Milford Sound

WEST COAST/
TE TAI POUTINI

Wild and beautiful, the West Coast extends for 600 kilometres between Kahurangi Point in the north and Awarua Point in the south. Midway between the towns of Westport and Greymouth, along the spectacular coastal road, is Punakaiki. The limestone formations here make up the famous Pancake Rocks and Blowholes — at their most impressive at high tide in a westerly sea.

Westport, at the mouth of the Buller River, was settled as a gold mining town in the 1860s and coal was discovered at the same time, establishing a more stable economy for the town. The port provides a protected haven for both fishing and leisure boats. South of Westport is Carters Beach, considered to be the only beach on the West Coast that is safe for swimming.

Continuing south, there is Tauranga Bay at Cape Foulwind, home to a New Zealand fur seal colony. Dolphins, orcas and occasionally southern right whales, can be seen in the surrounding sea.

South of Greymouth, is the third river-port town on the West Coast, Hokitika. The notorious 'Hokitika Bar' at the mouth of river shifts with every tide and has causes many ships to founder.

The southern West Coast with its five national parks, two kiwi sanctuaries and an awe-inspiring landscape has been named by UNESCO as a world heritage site.

Punakaiki

FISHING BOATS

1 Houhora, Northland
2 Inner harbour, Gisborne
3 Tauranga, Bay of Plenty
4 Jetty, Coromandel
5 Red-billed gulls, Oamaru
6 Riverton, Southland

Fishing boat, Westport

Next page: Cape Foulwind to the South of Carters Beach, Westport

Rapahoe Beach, just north of Greymouth
Opposite: Coastline, Hokitika

NEW ZEALAND
North Island

LEGEND

00 Page reference

Towns and cities

Major roads

Minor roads

Chapter boundaries

Please note that chapter boundaries are not official regional boundaries, simply a guide to this book

10 11 8 9

Cape Reinga

13
16
Kaitaia
Kerikeri   Bay of Islands
15 19

Hokianga
18
Northland

Whangarei

Dargaville

19

Kaipara Harbour

Great Barrier Island

29
23
Coromandel Peninsula
40 42

38 36
AUCKLAND
32 35 34
24 -27
20
Waiheke I
37 30 31
Auckland

46
White I
49

44
Tauranga
Hamilton
Bay of Plenty

48

Lake Rotorua
Rotorua

Waikato
Central Plateau and Thermal Region
East Cape
50

53 52
Gisborne

58
Taumarunui
Lake Taupo
Taupo

Hawkes Bay

56
61
New Plymouth
6 54

65
Mt Taranaki
Mt Ruapehu

Taranaki
57 Napier
Hastings

Wanganui
62
63
Manawatu

Palmerston North

66

Masterton

68 71 73 74
Wellington
WELLINGTON

Cook Strait

NEW ZEALAND
South Island

Farewell Spit

76
79 2 78
79
1 80
81 82
84
Abel Tasman
National Park
83
86 89
88 Picton
Nelson
6
121 Westport
Nelson Tasman
Marlborough
122
118
KaiKoura
6
Lewis
Pass
125
93
Greymouth
7
90 Kaikoura
West Coast
7
124 Hokitika
Arthur's
Pass
1
6
73
7
Canterbury and
MacKenzie Basin
96
Aoraki/Mt Cook
CHRISTCHURCH
97
Lake
Pukaki
Lake Tekapo
98 94
96
8
Akaroa
1
Lake
Hawea
Mt Aspiring
6
116 Milford Sound
Lake
Wanaka
8
Wanaka
Glenorchy
Arrowtown
85
Queenstown
Cromwell
Oamaru
1
Otago
105 Moeraki
Te Anau
8
1
102
6
100 103 4
Fiordland
Southland
106 DUNEDIN
8
104
112
1
113
108
Invercargill
Bluff
110
Foveaux Strait
Stewart Island
114
115
Stewart Island